FRANCE

BY
ROBIN TWIDDY

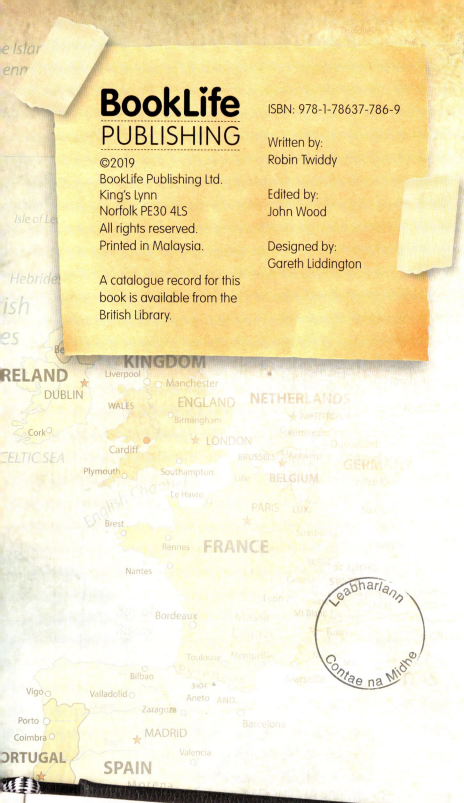

BookLife
PUBLISHING

©2019
BookLife Publishing Ltd.
King's Lynn
Norfolk PE30 4LS
All rights reserved.
Printed in Malaysia.

A catalogue record for this book is available from the British Library.

ISBN: 978-1-78637-786-9

Written by:
Robin Twiddy

Edited by:
John Wood

Designed by:
Gareth Liddington

Photocredits:

Cover – Naniti, Production Perig, Marques, Catarina Belova, dikobraziy, Alliance, onot, picturepartners, 4 - Alliance, rolandtopor, BurAnd, graja, 5 - Philip Lange, Shebeko, Mega Pixel, InnaFelker 6 - LongJon, BAKOUNINE, RinUm, 7 - Kiev.Victor, goga18128, Jessica2, george photo cm, 8 - Slepitsssskaya, SAHAS2015, 9 - VanoVasaio, kavram, 10 - Irina Popoyan, Lukas Buschoff Photograph, Anna Minsk, photographerstudio, 11 - Riska Parakeet, Michael Sheridan, Edward Westmacott, 12 - Belt944, AWP76, BOONCHUAY PROMJIAM, Sondre Lysne, 13 - Pierre Jean Durieu, Mirabelle Pictures, IDI974, Tony Stock, charl989, 14 - canadastock, gorillaimages, Big Foot Productions, Vova Shevchuk, 15 - YuG, HUANG Zheng, Billion Photos, 16 - Gijs Rijsdijk, visual12, Melok, Delpixel 17 - andre quinou, Martijn L, 18 - Viacheslav Lopatin, Tekkol, 19 - Viacheslav Lopatin, Alina Zamogilnykh, 20 - S.Borisov, Orapin Joyphuem, Maglara, 21 - Sebastiana, banicka, Nyvlt-art, 22 - anyaivanova, Resul Muslu, 23 - Takashi Images, Catarina Belova, Peyker, khuruzero, 24 - Mister_Knight, zef art, perfectlab, 25 - PhotoFires, geraria, Peter Hermes Furian, Triff, 26 - Lekchalit, Alessandro Colle, Volodymur Hlukhovskyi, 27 - Pack-Shot, Esposito Photography, photosoft, 30 - Fisman64, Croisy, S.Borisov.Images are courtesy of Shutterstock.com. With thanks to Getty Images, Thinkstock Photo and iStockphoto.

All facts, statistics, web addresses and URLs in this book were verified as valid and accurate at time of writing. No responsibility for any changes to external websites or references can be accepted by either the author or publisher.

CONTENTS

EUROSTA
DEPARTS
16:35

Words that look like this can be found in the glossary on page 31.

TRAIN TICKET
SINGLE
Seat: 12B
To: **PARIS**
T1234567890
Number: 1666
DATE: 14/09/
704

WELCOME TO FRANCE

Bonjour! That means hello in French. My name is Amelie. I live in Cannes in the south of France with my family. We are going on a road trip across France. There is so much to see – I can't wait.

Look out for coordinates in boxes like these. Use the internet to explore these places online. You can ask an adult to help you.

THE CURRENCY WE USE IN FRANCE IS THE EURO.

France is in the continent of Europe and is part of the European Union. My country shares borders with six other countries. These are Belgium, Luxembourg, Germany, Switzerland, Italy and Spain.

FRANCE

FRENCH CULTURE

France is really well known for its <u>culture</u> and food – especially its pastries, cheese and bread. We are also famous for our philosophers. That is a big word, but don't worry – it just means people who think and write about what life is and how to live.

PASTRIES

France has lots of different people from different countries, cultures and religions living in it.

ALL FRENCH CHILDREN LEARN SOME PHILOSOPHY IN SECONDARY SCHOOL.

THE CANNES FILM FESTIVAL

A BUSY CITY

Every year, one of the most famous film festivals in the world is held in Cannes. It is pretty amazing to see the city fill up with famous people. New films are shown at the festival and some of them win awards and prizes.

THE RED CARPET

The red carpet at the film festival is a great place to see some amazing fashion. All the film stars dress up in fancy clothes and have their pictures taken.

SOME PEOPLE CALL PARIS, THE CAPITAL OF FRANCE, THE FASHION CAPITAL OF THE WORLD.

CANNES

Cannes is on the French Riviera. That is the south-east coast. It gets really warm here in the summer. A lot of people visit Cannes on holiday for the beaches and sunshine.

THE MAN IN THE IRON MASK

My favourite thing about Cannes is the history. The islands of Lérins can be reached by boat from Cannes. One of the islands was a prison. Its most famous prisoner was the man in the iron mask.

I WONDER WHO THAT MASKED MAN WAS?

PONT DU GARD

Next we went to the Pont du Gard. This ancient aqueduct bridge is part of the Nîmes aqueduct, which was built in around <u>AD</u> 50 to carry water 50 kilometres to the Roman colony of Nemausus. A Roman colony was where lots of Romans lived together in a different country. It is amazing to think it was built almost 2,000 years ago.

AN AQUEDUCT IS A SPECIAL BRIDGE THAT CARRIES WATER FROM ONE PLACE TO ANOTHER.

PONT DU GARD COORDINATES
43.947065,
4.534821

It is one of the best Roman bridges in the world. Looking at the aqueduct, it is easy to imagine what France was like when the Romans lived here.

MUSEUM

At the Pont du Gard we visited the museum. You can learn all about how the aqueduct was built and how the Romans lived in ancient France.

I really liked visiting the Pont du Gard, but it is in the middle of nowhere and there isn't much else nearby. Next, we are going to visit Carcassonne, which is an amazing city. I can't wait!

CARCASSONNE

Carcassonne is incredible. It is a <u>medieval</u> walled city and it still looks almost exactly like it did when it was built. The walls are three kilometres long and there are 52 towers.

PEOPLE MUST HAVE FELT VERY SAFE LIVING BEHIND THESE WALLS.

CARCASSONNE COORDINATES
43.207550,
2.362933

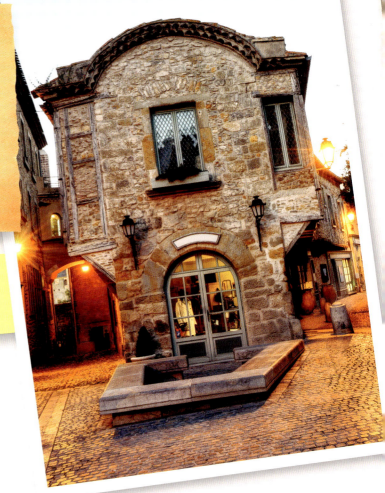

Walking around the city is like going back in time. But the amazing thing is that people still live here. You can walk into a building built hundreds of years ago and buy an ice cream.

This city has seen a lot of history, which you can learn about as you tour it. There are lots of amazing buildings in the city, but my favourite is the cathedral. It is called the Basilica of Saint-Nazaire and Saint-Celse.

THE CATHEDRAL WAS SUPER COOL. I REALLY LIKED THE GARGOYLES. I WONDER IF WE WILL SEE ANY MORE.

THE FOOD MARKET

Before we left the city, we visited the food market. In France we have lots of food markets where you can buy fresh local foods. There was local duck, pork and cheese for sale.

ROCAMADOUR

Rocamadour was amazing. There were places to camp and lots to do. First we visited the clifftop village. It is built right into the side of the cliff. Rocamadour is an important <u>Christian</u> religious site and people have been travelling there on <u>pilgrimages</u> for over a thousand years.

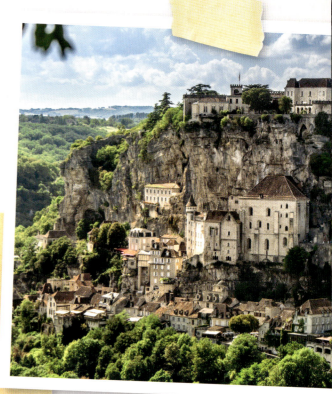

We also visited the bird sanctuary. There were all sorts of colourful birds to see, such as parrots, owls and vultures. They have birds from all around the world.

MONK VULTURE

DURANDAL MEDIEVAL SHOW

My favourite part of Rocamadour was the Durandal Medieval Show. There was horse riding with lots of sword fighting and stunts. It was really fun. It must be <u>très difficile</u>.

FAMOUS CHEESE

We tried some goat's cheese from the local market. The goat's cheese from this area is famous around the world. It was really good, but it was also really strong.

THE FRENCH ALPS

The Alps are a mountain range on the eastern border of France. Some of the mountains cross over into Italy and Switzerland. The Alps have snowy peaks, green forests and beautiful lakes.

I LOVE WALKING THROUGH THE MOUNTAINS.

SKIING

You can't come to the Alps without having a go at skiing – or at least that is what my dad says. I had never skied before but I got the hang of it in the end. Many people love to come to the French Alps to ski.

The tallest peak in the Alps is Mont Blanc which reaches around 4,800 metres high. People come from all over to climb it. In English, Mount Blanc means White Mountain.

MUM WANTED TO CLIMB IT, BUT DAD SAID IT WOULD TAKE TOO LONG. I DON'T THINK HE LIKES THE COLD.

HIKING

We went on a walk through the Alps. There are lots of hiking routes through the mountains. Some are really hard, and some are much easier. Walking through the Alps really lets you see how varied the French landscape can be.

BURGUNDY CANAL

In Burgundy we hired a boat and travelled along the <u>canal</u> system. Mostly people now use the canals for fun and holidays. When the Burgundy Canal was built it was really important. It joined the north and south of France together.

ALSO, IT IS REALLY RELAXING SITTING ON A CANAL BOAT IN THE SUN.

Before the canals it must have been really hard to transport things across the country. The canals made it possible for people to trade across the country.

People started building the canals in the late 1700s but they had to stop for around 15 years because of the <u>French Revolution</u>. It finally opened in 1832. Thanks to the canals you can see a lot of French history and countryside.

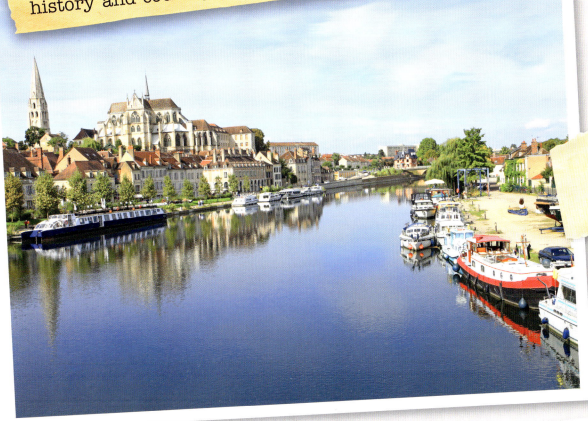

Burgundy is very pretty but the next stop is the capital city. We took the canals north and then took the Saône and the Rhône rivers to Paris. I don't think there is a better way to arrive in Paris.

I LIKED THE CANAL BOATS BUT SOMETIMES I WISHED WE COULD GO FASTER.

NOTRE-DAME

There is so much to see in Paris, but the first thing I wanted to see was the Notre-Dame Cathedral. Some people say that it is the best cathedral in France.

THE CATHEDRAL WAS BUILT BETWEEN 1163 AND 1245. THAT IS A LONG TIME AGO.

The Notre-Dame Cathedral is amazing. It is really big and when you go inside you can see why so many people visit it each year. It is the most-visited place in all of Paris.

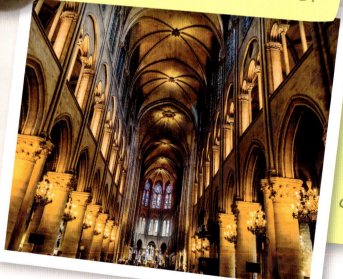

MUM SAYS THAT THE STYLE OF BUILDING IS CALLED GOTHIC. IN FRANCE, WE ARE FAMOUS FOR OUR GOTHIC BUILDINGS.

Notre-Dame Cathedral is the setting for one of my favourite stories, Victor Hugo's The Hunchback of Notre-Dame. In France the book is called Our Lady of Paris. Thanks to Victor Hugo, people travel from around the world to see this famous cathedral.

STAINED GLASS WINDOWS

SCULPTURES

INSIDE THE CATHEDRAL YOU CAN SEE ALL OF THE SCULPTURES AND STAINED GLASS WINDOWS. WOW!

If you climb the 387 steps to the top of the cathedral you will see an amazing sight. At the top of the cathedral are many gargoyles overlooking the city. Some look like demons and some look like birds or other animals.

EIFFEL TOWER

You shouldn't visit Paris without going to the Eiffel Tower. You can find it on the Champ de Mars. It is one of the most famous landmarks in the world and it is visited by millions of people every year.

THE EIFFEL TOWER LOOKS AMAZING AT NIGHT.

The Eiffel Tower is made from iron and is 320 metres tall. It was built in 1889 as part of the <u>World's Fair</u> celebrating 100 years since the French Revolution. When it was built, it was the tallest human-made object in the world.

TRAIN TICKET

SINGLE

DATE: 14/09/2018

Number: 1666

Seat: 12B

To: PARIS

T123456789

The Eiffel Tower was only supposed to last for 20 years, but it is now over 130 years old. If you travel to the top of the Eiffel Tower, you get an amazing view of Paris. It is no wonder so many people come here.

I FOUND OUT THAT THE TOWER CAN CHANGE HEIGHT UP TO 17 CENTIMETRES DEPENDING ON HOW HOT OR COLD IT IS. OH LA VACHE!

After visiting the Eiffel Tower, we stopped to get something to eat. I had a buttered croissant and a slice of lemon tart. C'était délicieux! Mum and Dad had herb-buttered snails. I don't really like snails, but they do.

THE LOUVRE

After the Eiffel Tower, we visited the Louvre. The Louvre is an art gallery and museum in Paris. It is huge. There is so much art and history to see in the Louvre, including some of the most famous paintings and sculptures in the world.

Art is an important part of French history and culture, and you can see a lot of it in the Louvre. Some of the most famous pieces of art in the world are kept there, including the Venus de Milo and the Mona Lisa.

IT WAS REALLY BUSY AT THE LOUVRE.

MONA LISA

There isn't just art in the Louvre. You can also find lots of historical objects from all around the world. The Louvre is actually the biggest art museum on the planet. It is so big that you can't see it all in one day. C'est grand!

THE RIVER SEINE

Before leaving Paris, we got some crêpes to eat whilst we walked along the banks of the Seine. That is the river that runs through Paris. It is just behind the Louvre. I think a boat trip down the Seine would be something very special.

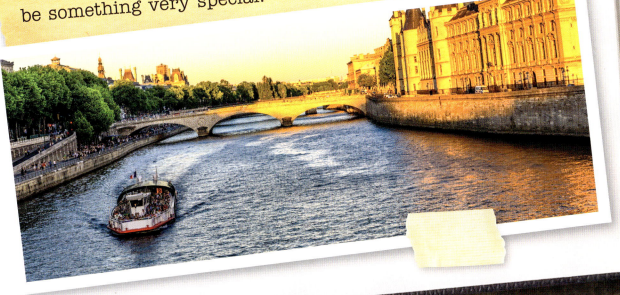

PALACE OF VERSAILLES

France hasn't had a royal family for a very long time but when we did, they lived here in the Palace of Versailles. We went on the tour and it was amazing. I have never seen so much gold.

This is where the king and queen, Louis XVI and Marie Antoinette, lived before they were captured and executed during the French Revolution. Louis XVI and Marie Antoinette were beheaded with a <u>guillotine</u> in 1793.

The Palace of Versailles is one of the biggest out of all palaces and castles in the world. You could spend all day just walking round the gardens. There is a lot of French history in this palace.

I CAN'T IMAGINE WHAT IT WOULD BE LIKE TO LIVE IN A PALACE LIKE THIS. I THINK I WOULD GET LOST A LOT.

When we were at the palace, we tried some cakes fit for royalty. I had some mille-feuille. It was really nice. I wonder if Marie-Antionette liked this type of cake?

MILLE-FEUILLE

D-DAY LANDING SITE

One of the saddest parts of French history is when the <u>Nazis</u> invaded France in the Second World War. The last stop on our journey is to the beaches that our <u>allies</u> landed on to help fight back.

On the 6th of June, 1944 thousands of allied troops from the UK, the USA and Canada stormed the beaches of Normandy. You can still see a lot of the German defences.

THIS SIGN CAN BE FOUND ON OMAHA BEACH.

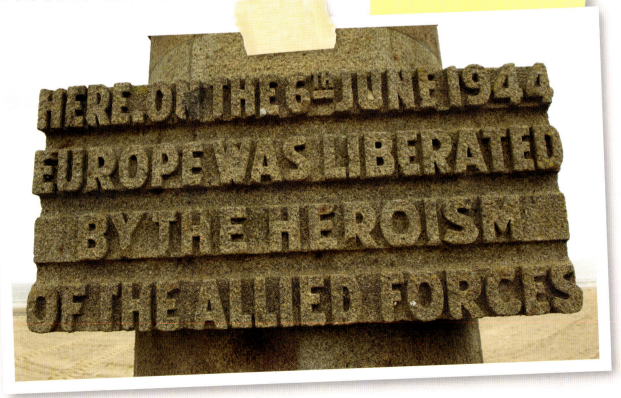

HERE, ON THE 6th JUNE 1944 EUROPE WAS LIBERATED BY THE HEROISM OF THE ALLIED FORCES

There is a lot of information about the D-Day landings and how they helped win the war. We hired bikes so that we could get between the different beaches and see as much as possible.

This is a really important part of our history, and all of Europe's too. I am glad we came to see it. After the D-Day landings, the allied troops and the <u>French Resistance</u> fought for nearly three months to <u>liberate</u> France.

WHEN THE FIGHTING WAS OVER, THE BELLS AT THE NOTRE-DAME CATHEDRAL RANG OUT TO CELEBRATE.

27

THE JOURNEY

Look at all the places we have visited on our journey.

LET THEM EAT CAKE!

PALACE OF VERSAILLES

D-DAY LANDING

ROCAMADOUR

CARCASSONNE

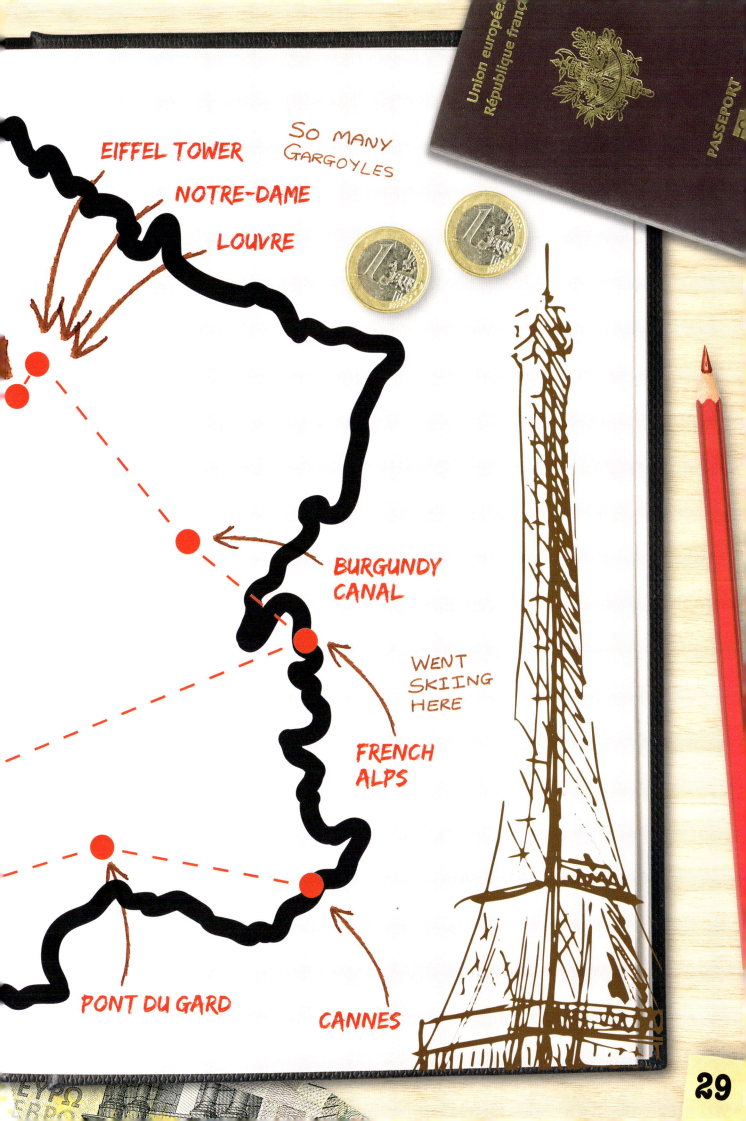

AU REVOIR

Au revoir! Je me suis bien amusée travelling around France with my family. I have learnt so much about my own country and its history. There were so many beautiful old towns and buildings.

I think my favourite things, except for the cakes, were the gargoyles. I would like to go back to the Louvre. There was so much that we didn't have time to see.

GLOSSARY

AD	after the birth of Jesus, which is used as the starting point for many calendars around the world
allies	groups who are on the same side
au revoir	goodbye
borders	the edges of a country or object
c'était délicieux	it was delicious
c'est grand	it's big
canal	a river-like body of water made by humans for transport
Christian	related to or concerning the religion of Christianity
crêpes	thin pancakes
culture	the way of life and traditions of a group of people
currency	the type of money used in a particular country
French Resistance	a group of people who formed in secret during the Second World War to fight against the Nazis
French Revolution	when the people of France fought against the monarchy and the rich
guillotine	a means of executing people (by cutting off their heads)
je me suis bien amusée	I had fun
landscape	all the land that can be seen
liberate	to free or let out
medieval	the period of time from the 11th century to the 14th century
Nazis	a group of people that controlled Germany from 1933 to 1945 and fought in World War Two
oh la vache	holy cow
pilgrimages	long trips undertaken for religious purposes
très difficile	very difficult
World's Fair	an international festival of scientific and technological achievements

INDEX